C000147364

SNOWDOMES

Series editor: Frédérique Crestin-Billet
Design by Lélie Carnot
Typesetting by Special Edition Pre-press Services
Translated from the French by Chet Wiener and Stacy Doris
Copy-edited by Corinne Orde
Originally published as La Folie des Boules à Neige
© 2001 Flammarion, Paris
This English-language edition © 2002 Flammarion Inc.

ISBN: 2-0801-0889-1
Printed in France

Collectible
SNOWDOMES

Lélie Carnot

Flammarion

The beauty of collections that stay in the family is the view that each successive generation brings to bear. From great-grandparents to great-grandchildren, with all the stages in-between, if the collections of family members from each era can stand side by side, as they do in some cases where the passion seems to get handed down, what a celebration of tastes and interests will ensue! It often happens that the youngest family members are the ones who are the most fascinated by the knick-knacks of their ancestors, while those closest in age don't quite seem to comprehend each others' tastes. It is for this reason that it is best to keep your heart and mind open, as well as your eyes. Collectors know that time will tell.

CONTENTS

Introduction

The urge is overwhelming. And the magic effect? Instant gratification. Who can resist the temptation of picking up one of these smooth, rounded domes, perhaps tentatively the first time, and overturning the little universe under the glass? You wait a while, and then you turn it back to its proper position. Suddenly, as if you were playing god, or a television weather anchor at least, you see that you've created a snowstorm of white flakes softly floating down while you stand safe and sound, holding the world in the palm of your hand. Then, as if you didn't quite believe your eyes the first time around, you do it again and watch the snowflakes swirling as they gently come to rest.

INTRODUCTION

Snowdomes, snowglobes, paperweights, snow machines, or just plain "shaky things," as many call them; dreamglobes, *Traümkegel* or "dream balls" in German: as with any new field of technology, the terminology has not yet been fixed with strict precision. The history of snowdomes, as they are referred to throughout this book, is equally difficult to pin down. Some claim that they descend from the heavy glass paperweights sometimes known in England as "sulfides." These thick glass balls were invented in Venice, Italy, around 1850. They typically englobe cut strips of kaleidoscopic millefiori glass, or cameos, or various incrustations, and are beautiful, fascinating, and precious. Sulfide and millefiori paperweights were popular with collectors in the second half of the eighteenth century, but their costly materials and manufacture kept them off limits to the general public, for whom the snowdome may have been invented. Snowdomes also provided an added excitement: they were dynamic in that they had miraculous tumbling snowflakes.

The likely ancestors of today's snowdome are these heavy antique millefiori paperweights, which are far more costly.

INTRODUCTION

The first mention of snowdomes in writing may well have been in the official American report on the Paris Exposition of 1878. Among the 52,835 exhibits in the immense exhibition spaces, according to Charles Cole, the Deputy Secretary of the Commission for Glassware, were "paperweights, in the form of hollow balls filled with water, containing a man with an umbrella. These balls also contain a white powder that, when the paperweight is turned over, produces a snowfall." While the description is clear and precise, nothing is said about the manufacturer or the country of origin. In this sense, as in many others, the snowdome is truly international. One thing is certain about the earliest snowdomes: they were pretty heavy. In addition to the weight of the water and glass, there was the base, which could be

This painted porcelain lighthouse in its glass egg stands on a ceramic base. The water has largely evaporated with time. The snow, which could be composed of a variety of materials (see page 157), is no longer white.

made of ceramic, brass, or even marble. Their heaviness helped them to serve their attributed function as paperweights. Eleven years after Cole's citing, back in Paris again but this time for the 1889 Exposition, thirty-three million visitors came to marvel at the steel structure that had been erected especially for the occasion by the engineer Gustave Eiffel. This was, of course, none other than the Eiffel Tower, which, by popular demand, was left standing after the show, and so it remains to this day. It is hard to imagine that this great marketing opportunity would have been missed by the snowdome makers of the time, but there are no extant Eiffel Tower souvenir snowdomes to prove it conclusively. Nevertheless, some Eiffel Tower snowdomes do suggest that they date from the time of its inauguration.

This 1940s porcelain Eiffel Tower snowdome resembles late nineteenth-century models.

By the beginning of the twentieth century, the manufacturers of souvenirs in Austria, France, Germany, Czechoslovakia, and elsewhere were featuring snowdomes in their sales catalogs. Religious subjects with links to important pilgrimage sites seem to have been the most popular. Among them were Saint Theresa of Lisieux, and Saint Bernadette of Lourdes, both canonized in the 1920s, Saint Anthony of Padua, Our Lady of Czestochowa, in Poland, and the miraculous statuette of the Infant Jesus, known as the Holy Child of Prague.

While they were widely available to the general public during the first decades of the twentieth century, snowdomes cannot claim to have been all the rage. In fact, in the numerous department store

The Virgin Mary appears in a vision to Bernadette of Lourdes in this well-made glass snowglobe on a ceramic base.

catalogs still preserved from the period, there is not a single mention of a snowdome for sale. Nor are any pictured in the imaginative and varied publicity images of the time. Looking through these brochures, you can find countless paperweights, bookends, all conceivable types of desk accessory, glowing globes of the earth, sparkling Virgin Marys, every sort of porcelain animal in creation, and figurines in regional dress. All of these items are popular subjects for snowdomes, yet the domes themselves were missing. They were omitted too from the toy and gift catalogs of the time, which abound in Santa Claus candles and folkloric dolls.

*A recently minted series of Swiss
stamps shows the most typical
national snowdome subjects.*

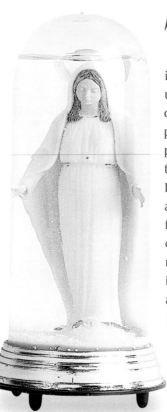

The real snowdome boom got underway in the late 1940s. Two factors led to this explosion of interest. The first was the ever-increasing use of plastic, which allowed for all kinds of whims to be executed for a reasonable price. The second was the growing prevalence of paid vacations, which led to the development of the tourist industry. For those who could now afford to travel and were able to take their families away for a few days' holiday, souvenirs were in order. As if in response to this new market, the snowdome became lighter in weight and adopted a colorful base and a broader range of subjects. The paperweight idea went by the wayside.

The Virgin Mary was a prevailing snowdome subject in the early twentieth century, and she remains popular today, a century later. This recent Italian-made Virgin glows in the dark.

T wo German manufacturers made major contributions to the development of snowdomes: Koziol and Walter & Prediger. They were embroiled in a court case over the invention of the dome shape. Otto Walter and Alfred Prediger had been in business making girls' hair accessories since 1847. They hit on the idea of placing their stock of surplus barrette figurines, which were paintend on one side only, into clear oval-shaped balls with painted blue backgrounds. The color produced a sort of magical effect on the little objects contained within balls, but it also served the practical purpose of masking the undecorated side of the tableau. Around the same time, Bernhard Koziol, who went into the souvenir business in 1927, was watching a snowstorm through the rear window of his car when he had

*Kitsch meets kitsch in this sculpture snowdome.
A definite collector's item for the future.*

For this tiny sponge cake under glass made by the German manufacturer Koziol, the snow doubles as a tasty sugar coating.

the brainwave of making dome-shaped snowglobes. It was the distinctive shape of the glass in the window that inspired him to create the dome. However, the courts did not find in his favor. Henceforth Koziol would be prohibited from using the dome shape for his souvenirs and would only be allowed to manufacture goods that used the spherical form. In the end, however, Koziol used this limitation to his advantage, and the trademark globe form at which he excels became a major factor in setting his company a cut above the rest, to this day.

Some collectors like to focus on objects that incorporate snowdome concepts. Here are just a few among hundreds: key rings, pins, and even a folding umbrella with a snowdome handle.

O ne of the few patents in the history of snowdome manufacture was granted in the United States in 1927 to one Joseph Garaja. But the production of snowdomes didn't really get going in earnest in the States until the 1940s. Between 1941 and 1949, the now legendary Atlas Crystal Works churned out thousands of models. The brand was taken over by the World Art Studio, which nowadays specializes in commemorative plaques. Unfortunately, the entire archives of Atlas Crystal Works were lost in a series of floods. A more recent American manufacturer, equally important among snowdome collectors, is Enesco, which started production in 1958. An innovative

This giant snowdome, containing the main monuments of Paris, was part of the city's 1993 outdoor Christmas display. An idea worth a repeat performance.

spearhead of the gift and gadget industry, Enesco now has branches and affiliates in Canada, Great Britain, Germany, Australia, Hong Kong, and elsewhere. Another major snowdome player is the Silvestri Corporation. Specializing in festive goods and decorations for the Christmas season, it is a major importer of foreign-made snowdomes from Europe, the Philippines, Taiwan, China, India, and Korea. In the 1970s, several Asian nations, including China and Hong Kong, took over the bulk of snowdome manufacturing. This led to a

Some snowdome subjects are specifically made for particular monuments, sites, or occasions. Others are more generic and can be used for different circumstances. The unpainted molds on the left and the painted ones on the right, both from the French manufacturer Convert, show some of the designs available.

largely unregulated market in which models were freely and unashamedly copied with scant regard for licensing laws or copyright issues. The latter were circumvented by changing a color here or altering a small detail there. The Asian-made models are mainly destined for consumption in the West. In 1969, Convert, a French manufacturer, entered the snowdome market and opened a production plant in an area of France in which the manufacture of celluloid and plastic products was already well established. The firm specializes in souvenir models for the tourist industry. Pierre Convert, the company's current director, launched a campaign to promote the use of snowdomes in advertising. It met with limited success, but the results can make for an interesting snowdome collection.

Advertising agencies may design imaginary snowdomes (facing page). Sometimes, they become a reality (left).

J' ♥ CUISINES TEISSEIRE

faire du ciel le p

MOSKVA

BADOIT

BADOIT

Souvenir de S.t Galmier

GODIN

A revival of interest in snowdomes over the past twenty years has led the market itself to turn on its head! Quality is on the rise, and ordinary buyers—not just the collectors—have become much more discriminating. In response, many manufacturers are going back to using glass domes and balls, wooden bases, and high-relief figurines and scenes. At the same time, advances in plastics and materials technology have made it possible to produce models that look just as good as those made from the more expensive natural materials. They are certainly far more convincing than earlier attempts. And the new synthetic compounds have the advantage of being much sturdier and longer lasting than their predecessors.

The snowdome form inspired this paper perfume sample of Fragile *(above), a fragrance by Jean-Paul Gaultier that comes in a snowdome-shaped bottle.*

This limited edition Christmas watch by Swatch has a snowdome for the face.

T he snowdome's appeal may lie in offering a whole little universe that can fit in the palm of your hand. Or maybe it is the sight of the snow, softly and silently coming to rest on the miniature scene. As in other fields, collections have often begun almost by chance, with the acquisition of first one example, then another to make a pair, and then a third. After that, the urge to pick up yet another snowdome becomes hard to resist. With the help of a few strategic globe-trotting friends, you can get a fine collection going in no time—each specimen evoking a special yet varied, colorful and somehow childlike universe, a small world that is safe and enclosed. I only hope you will take as much delight in peeping through the windows on the following pages as I have.

Popularity and innovation have at times led snowdomes to lose their classic shapes. The treasure-chest model goes along with snowdome televisions, aquariums, bottles, and other variations.

I

FIGURATIVE

snowdomes

Famous or anonymous, celestial or terrestrial, many a figure has been memorialized under glass over the years, with snowstorms raging over their heads for ever more. Religious subjects were popular in the early twentieth century, and continue to be today. But the blessed Virgins and serene saints immortalized in their heavenly spheres soon faced competition from more earthly candidates. Men, women, and children proudly proclaimed their cultural origins in colorful traditional costume. Then athletes, soldiers, rock singers, movie stars, and celebrities of all kinds earned a place in these wintry microcosms. Here then is a picture gallery where you may encounter some unexpected faces.

Saint Theresa of Lisieux is a snowdome favorite. Her popularity spread throughout the world following her death on September 30, 1897. She was beatified in 1923 and canonized two years later, at a time that miraculously coincided with the first growth spurt of snowdome souvenirs.

You can distinguish Saint Theresa from other saints by the roses that always surround her. In her writings, she referred to the miracles, healings, and conversions she foresaw as a "shower of roses." The two snowdomes shown here are from the same manufacturer and feature a similar pose in different color schemes.

Thérèse Martin entered the convent of Lisieux, in France, at the age of fifteen. During her brief periods of respite from the rigors of the religious life she was said to have been blessed with a sunny nature and a light-hearted disposition. This pose in a pool of dark rosewater would doubtless have appealed to her sense of humor.

Thanks to Saint Theresa, Lisieux has been a pilgrimage destination for over a century. A million and a half pilgrims make their way there each year. Between 1898 and 1925, more than thirty million images of the saint were sold, but the sales figures for Theresa snowdomes are not known. The calendar on this one suggests that it was intended for English-speaking visitors.

Many snowdomes also bear witness to the popularity of Bernadette Soubirous, another saint. She had no fewer than eighteen visions of the Virgin Mary. This 1958 model commemorates the centenary of Bernadette's first vision, on February 11, 1858.

This best-selling Bernadette scene shows her vision of the Virgin in the crevice of a rock in Lourdes, France. Mary's words to Bernadette, "I am the Immaculate Conception," are printed on the banner.

Whether faulty filling
or evaporation is
responsible, the water
level in snowdomes
often manages to settle
exactly on a line with a
figure's face, usually at
eye level, making it
hard to see the features
under the magnifying
dome. That is why this
Virgin is shown here in a
somewhat undignified
position.

When they contain such
figures from Christianity,
elongated snowdomes can
call to mind the taper candles
found in churches. This one,
like the model to the left,
even glows in the dark.

In Italy there is a tradition of mounting snowdomes on pedestals of shells. Here, the shells have cracked, and the paint inside has flaked to the point where it is hard to say whether we have the Virgin Mary or a saint. The overall blurred effect is melancholy and mysterious.

The cloudy atmosphere in the model on the left is due to the blue paint on the dome diluting in the liquid. In this model, the paint is better preserved, giving an overall blue glow. The figure wielding a patriotic flag may be Saint Catherine of Sienna, who, jointly with Francis of Assisi, is the patron saint of Italy.

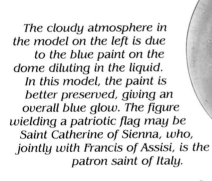

Black Virgins are usually wooden statues that started life a paler color but darkened over time as a result of exposure to dust and candle soot. Some of them may have blackened as a result of having been buried away for several centuries. The maker of this snowdome obviously decided to take the idea one step farther!

Black Virgins are popular international snowdome subjects. Below left, seated in a grove of bananas, is Candelaria of Tenerife, the patron saint of the Spanish Canary Islands. On the right, a small dome encloses the Madonna of Tindari, commemorated every year in Sicily on September 7 and 8.

The faces of this poor
Virgin and Child seem
blinded by a tidal
wave. What could
have possessed them
to go wandering
among these toxic-
looking Christmas
trees, in this unusual,
cube-shaped dome?

This Italian Madonna and Child seem much more cozy and at home, crowned on their throne of puffy clouds. The majestic décor, all in warm reds and yellows, is painted on the inside of the globe, which sits on an elaborate shell base.

The crucifixion scene on the left was made in Germany, and faithfully shows the twelfth station of the cross. A collector would immediately wonder if other stations were represented in the same series. The snowdome to the right was made in China and has Christ curiously placed in the middle of a lush green forest.

Saint Anthony of Padua was born in Portugal, but beloved in Italy. Here, he stands with baby Jesus in his arms, before his namesake basilica in Padua. This beautiful building, with its characteristic Byzantine-style domes, was built between the thirteenth and the sixteenth centuries.

This memento of the miracle of Pontmain is something of an oddity. The Virgin Mary appeared to some children in this French town in 1871. While the figure here certainly resembles the Virgin, it is hard to imagine why she appears with a metal bucket-like object on her head.

The enigmatic appeal of this "souvenir of Pompeii" is actually due to the poor quality of the materials that were used in its making. The plastic sphere has yellowed with age and is losing its shape to the left, and the paint inside has chipped and is falling away. The souvenir will surely not last as long as the ancient city that it commemorates.

Pope John Paul II was so often on the move that if there were a snowdome made for each stop on every one of his world tours, they would fill a whole room. This one was made for one of his trips to France in 1980.

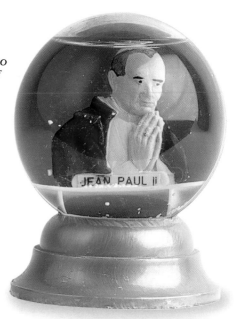

Despite her pursed, made-up lips and dramatically penciled eyebrows, this lady is nevertheless a nun, poring over her book in a snowstorm. Hopefully the wimple is protecting her head from the elements.

Like Theresa of Lisieux, Joan of Arc is one of the patron saints of France. Here she is on horseback, in front of the Cathedral of Orléans, in the city of her victorious battle of 1429. Also like Theresa, Joan was canonized at the time when snowdomes really began to take off. This helps to explain why so many Joan snowdomes still exist.

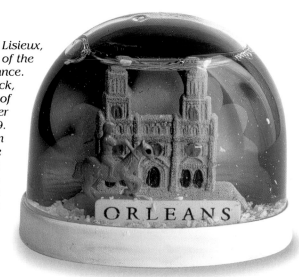

Enter stage right: Joan again, this time in the market square in Rouen, where she was burned at the stake in 1431. Though her facial expression is hidden by the bubbly water line, the proud white horse and raised banner seem to proclaim her innocence.

A series of related snowdomes can be made to have the effect of a comic strip. The Chinese calligrapher on this page scratches his head in search of inspiration. To the right, his face lights up as he hits on just the right idea. Note how he sets about preparing his ink. In the third episode, he is hard at work, with an expression of intense concentration. The snow in these domes is not white but is made from tiny golden flakes.

This pair of snowdomes is top-quality, with glass globes and beautifully crafted solid bases. They could almost stand in as snapshots from a society wedding album! To the left, the newlyweds have their first romantic dance as man and wife.

And on this page, the happy couple set off for their honeymoon in an open-topped automobile. Both of these snowdomes double as music boxes, for a touch of added romantic bliss. And instead of snow there is glittering wedding confetti raining on their shoulders.

First comes love, then comes marriage, and then... This angelic baby comes complete with a halo and might double as some sort of Christmas angel, popping out of a poinsettia patch.

Her sibling counterpart might be a mischievous tyke like this one, flinging his peas and carrots all over the place in an anti-vegetarian tantrum. The feisty little fellow was made in China, in 1994.

This kiddy comes in a snowdome that has a removable stopper in its pedestal for refills. But take care: the feature should only be used sparingly, since after the stopper has been removed two or three times it never quite fits back into its hole as well as it did to start with. This model was manufactured in Hong Kong.

The serious-looking little saxophonist is, for all his expression of child-like determination, unfortunately mounted on a fragile Plexiglas pedestal that is really too lightweight to support such a heavy glass ball. The rarity of such models testifies to their fragility.

The famous young prankster of Brussels, the Manneken-Pis, is doing his thing right in the central town square, not far from where the statue still stands. The original version was made by the sculptor Jerome Duquesnoy back in 1619. He could never have imagined that his subject would be transformed into cork-screws, cigarette lighters, dolls, and even snowdomes!

BRUSSELS

*Straight out of Hans Christian Andersen's tale, this
Little Mermaid is as representative an emblem of
Copenhagen as the Manneken-Pis is of Brussels.
Perched on her rock in the harbor, she has been
gazing out to sea since 1913.*

This little skier, a regular boy leprechaun with his green stocking cap and mittens, is a generic winter vacation souvenir. All you need to do is change the name. It could even be done with stickers, but that ruins all the fun of starting a collection.

More original is this child chimney sweep, whose hat looks leprechaun-like too. Given the dangers of his profession, maybe it is a good-luck hat. In the sooty days of the industrial revolution, the job was done mainly by children, their small size and their agility being considered advantages.

The missing sticker changes this winter trip souvenir into a generic homage to the sport of ski jumping. The date is unknown, too, though the figure's clothing and the manufacturing technique point to the 1960s.

Snowboarding is a more recent development, and this graceful athlete seems more advanced and up to date in every way—except for the place name, roughly scribbled on the base with a magic marker. How long before it rubs off?

Lélex is a ski destination in France, not far from Geneva and the Swiss border. This couple seem perfectly content inside their lean-to chalet after a good day on the slopes. They've planted their skis just outside and while they warm up. The figure on the left is smoking a pipe - quite an achievement under water.

LELEX

With a horn dangling at hip level, this alpine night watchman holds a heavy metal-tipped club in one hand. in the other hand—instead of the lantern you might think essential to his work—he holds a bottle, the contents of which he is rapidly draining, no doubt to keep warm in the cold night air.

Is a melted snowman, like the groundhog, one of the harbingers of spring? Who can resist a chuckle at the sight of this upturned hat floating in water? The carrot nose and coal eyes that once adorned the New York Snowman now lie forlornly on the ground.

MELTED
NEW YORK SNOWMAN

The idea of a snowman in California, melted or otherwise, is even more amusing. These companion pieces actually come from different manufacturers: A.C. Enterprises dreamed up the New York version, and the other is anonymously produced. But which came first?

Horse races and steeple-chases have been run in the French town of Pompadour ever since Syrian thoroughbreds were brought back from the Crusades. King Louis XV also gave the town's name to his mistress, the Marquise of Pompadour, who was born Antoinette Poisson.

For a more practical equestrian application, here is a member of the famous Royal Canadian Mounted Police in all his glory. Sadly, the horse's sleek black coat is seriously shedding its hairs and adding black flecks to the white snowflakes.

This diminutive violet seller of Toulouse, France, stands before the landmark Capitole building. Her straw hat is in keeping with traditional regional dress, but her grandiose skirt and cloak seem better suited to a formal ball. And where is her basket of flowers?

The prettily elongated dome seems specially designed to accommodate the tall head dress of this girl sporting the regional costume of Sables-d'Olonne, in the Vendée region of France. The traditional dress is readily identifiable by the short skirt and the towering headwear, which is perhaps slightly exaggerated here. This snowdome dates from 1940. Even back then, regional dress was only worn for certain festive occasions.

With its long tail, black spots, and what look like udders, this Chinese-made animal has something of a cow and something of a dog in its demeanor! In fact, it is supposed to represent a type of pig specially bred to sniff out truffles, those precious mushrooms. Notice the pointy snout.

The Auvergne is one of France's most untamed regions, with a rugged landscape of volcanoes and forests. In their regional dress worn for such occasions, the locals perform a traditional dance, either to celebrate a holiday, or for the benefit of tourists, or both. This snowdome was made in China.

*A generic French sailor, with a red pompom
on his cap, stands by the harbor wall in
front of his ship. The letters, hard to make
out in this picture, spell out the town of
Toulon. Otherwise, it could represent any
number of French military ports.*

*In this heavy snowstorm, it is just possible to see
the soldiers, marching to the sound of a trumpet.
They could be soldiers from the First World War, or
maybe British colonial troops. One thing is for sure,
they have a hard road ahead in that snowstorm.*

Square-shaped domes are far less common, and less popular, than round ones. But the extra room was probably needed to turn this tableau of Normandy peasants into a hoop game. The idea is to get the rings to go around the couple's bodies. Individually, it seems.

Colorful Alsatian costumes are often collectors' items in their own right; not only for snowdome collectors. The red color of the woman's dress is traditionally reserved for Catholics. A Protestant Alsatian woman would be wearing green, but I've not managed to find one represented in a snowdome.

The proper term for a Beefeater, whose job it is to guard the Tower of London, is Yeoman Warder. In his oblong dome, he is one of a series that includes the Horse Guard, minus his mount (facing page), and the Foot Guard, with his telltale bear-skin helmet (far right). This group also includes a regular policeman and a Welshman. But it doesn't seem complete without representatives from Scotland and Northern Ireland. About fifteen years ago, you could pick these fellows up at Lewis Nesson very cheaply.

The dome of this model is midway between the tapered style (see page 39) and the classic oval shape. Not to be confused with the British, the figures represented here are from Brittany, a region on the west coast of France rich in customs and traditions. The Pont-l'Abbé dress is rendered with a degree of faithful detail, despite the somewhat sketchy rendering of the features on the figures.

Different traditional costumes correspond to the different parts of Brittany. The men are wearing the blue glazik *of the Quimper area. The woman on the left wears a* bigouden *head dress from Pont-l'Abbé, while the head dress of the one on the right resembles those from Finistère. In short, this snowdome offers a little tour of the province under glass.*

The models on these two pages represent a new generation of snowdomes. Instead of containing three-dimensional scenes produced from molds, they use flat printed plastic strips on which the image is affixed by means of a technique similar to that used in the decoration of porcelain. These snowdomes don't have quite the same charm, but they are much cheaper to produce.

As a consequence, these snowdomes can be produced in runs of small quantities, which adds the appeal of rarity for collectors. It also means that a greater degree of personalization is possible. Another plus for both manufacturers and collectors is that the same image can be used to decorate a whole range of different items, from thermometers to coffee mugs, and everything in between.

*The little Dutch children in this dome dating from the 1960s
wear the regional dress of Volemdam, near Edam, but the
costume has come to represent all of the Netherlands.
The seesaw actually moves up and down. As for the rabbit
in the girl's arms, perhaps it swings in the balance.*

Holland is famous for its cheeses. This stocky little peasant woman, weighed down by the yoke on her shoulders, is carrying milk to make delicious Gouda. The miniature snowdome sits atop a pencil sharpener.

Small dome for tiny town and big dome for large country. The dimensions of the snowdome on the left are in keeping with the size of Ronda itself, the small southern Spanish town it commemorates, with its breathtaking aqueduct straddling a dramatic gorge. Spain, the country itself, deserves the bigger dome on the right.

The contents of the domes are identical. Even the photographic backgrounds are the same, except that the one on the left is slightly trimmed. The faces in the larger model are painted in, while the faces of the smaller couple are left without features.

ESPAÑA

This cheerful Tyrolean couple's expressions are cut off for now by the descending liquid level. Perhaps they are blinded by love. In a few years, once evaporation has done its work, we'll be able to look them in the eyes and decide.

Auberge means inn in French, but you won't be able to stay at the Auberge de Castille in Malta. Built to shelter the knights of the Order of Malta, it is now the official residence of the island's prime minister.

With the famous
bell-tower and basilica
of Bruges in the
background, this
happy crew is
enjoying a
motorboat ride on
the city's canals.
The picturesque
Belgian town
has been called
the Venice of
the North
because of its
abundant
waterways.

Still, there is a certain Italian romance to the real Venice that can't be beat, especially when it comes to a nocturnal gondola ride on the Grand Canal. The beauty of Venice has attracted many a tourist, which has in turn led to numerous snowdome versions of the city. You can see another one on page 153.

Water-skiing makes for classic snowdome subject matter. In keeping with the established tradition, the skier is mounted on a seesaw that moves when the snow-dome is shaken. But now that the paint has discolored, this water-skier seems to be stuck on some plowed field in the middle of the Great Plains.

This water-skiing couple has a more maritime backdrop, though the absence of a boat makes their activity seem somewhat ambiguous. They could just as easily be windsurfing, but where is the sail? Or perhaps, despite their appearance of grasping an invisible cord, they have tried out newfangled self-powered water skis, with no boat needed.

Martinique is a tropical paradise, complete with palm trees, turquoise waters, and a distant mountain. This dream tableau could appeal to anyone, in fact, if it weren't for the thought of snowflakes when you're wearing a bikini—especially such a diminutive one! But that's the fun of it all. And they don't call them snowdomes for nothing.

"Let it snow, let it snow, let it snow," as the song goes. These natives of Martinique don't seem to mind the snowstorm any more than the water-skier did. What is more, concentrating on playing their drums, they don't even seem to notice.

This tapered snowdome souvenir of the Emerald Isle, Ireland, is something less than majestic. A mournful family is drawn in their little open carriage in the snow. But even the snowflakes seem meager in size; more akin to raindrops. Maybe they are headed somewhere more cheerful.

There's no comparison between the poor Irish family and the almost opulent outfittings of this Scotsman in his bubble. The kilt, the tartan scarf, the jacket, and even the socks are finely detailed, and the bagpipes are splendid. The elaborate pedestal, with its craggy winding path to the castle's entrance, is as big as the globe it supports. The quality manufacturing of this recent piece is a sign of the current resurgence of interest in snowdomes.

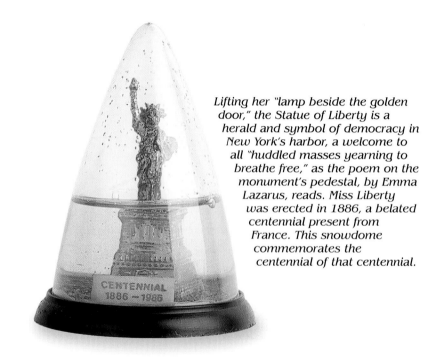

Lifting her "lamp beside the golden door," the Statue of Liberty is a herald and symbol of democracy in New York's harbor, a welcome to all "huddled masses yearning to breathe free," as the poem on the monument's pedestal, by Emma Lazarus, reads. Miss Liberty was erected in 1886, a belated centennial present from France. This snowdome commemorates the centennial of that centennial.

Queen Nefertiti of Ancient
Egypt is even better known
than her pharaoh husband,
Akhenaten. This fourteenth-
century BC monarch changed
the official religion to one of
the earliest known forms of
monotheism. On a more
down-to-earth level, note
the blue-tinted color of
the dome.

Seafaring themes make popular snowdome subjects. On this page, the red-haired buccaneer shoulders a cask of rum, his black-masted ship silhouetted in the background. On the facing page, left, these pirates don't look all that ferocious, lined up to make faces in front of their square-rigged vessel. To the right, the captain with his pipe waxes philosophical. He is probably waiting for the storm to abate before setting sail.

Is this just your everyday fisherman? Or an illustration of the fairy tale, "The Fisherman's Wife"? If so, maybe one of his three wishes should be to get a line for his fishing pole. Otherwise, both man and wife may starve before the trouble begins.

The fishing line is much in evidence here, as is all the gear, including net and basket. Yet the fisherman seems a bit impatient. Maybe he is waiting for the snow to stop. It is well known that fish bite in the rain, but are they as friendly when it snows?

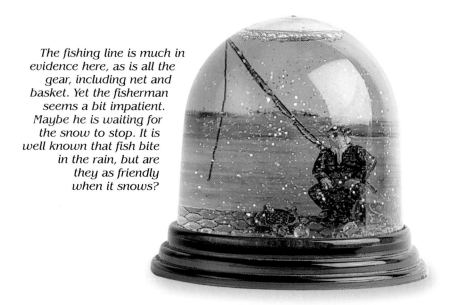

This grape picker must be in a region where the harvest comes unusually late. That explains the snow. In fact, such grape-growing areas do exist. But the snowglobe's base, which might have shed some light on the exact location, is unfortunately missing.

While you can get away with harvesting some white grapes so late that they have already dried out on the vine, it would be a crime to try that with the precious Pinot Noir grapes in the vineyards of Burgundy. This vine-grower has brought a barrel with him into the vineyards for inspiration.

This must be one of those show-off chefs, the kind that is so proud of his succulent free-range chicken that he can't keep himself from showing it to us before cooking it. Unless he wants us to eat it raw, that is. But his eyesight is cut off by the water level, so maybe it is an honest mistake.

This diligent chef has a big, old-fashioned cast-iron stove to be proud of. He is hard at work preparing a dish of asparagus. And in this dome it's not snow that rains down, it's a shower of vegetables.

The golfer seems to be concentrating as deeply as the chef, but he is no expert. You can tell by the clods of earth that fall down on him instead of snowflakes. The figurine, though, is carefully crafted, with nice, clear detailing. A luxury for snowdomes, the back view is also decorated, so you can study the player's swings from all angles.

Plenty of fine detailing went into this golfer, too, but you can't analyze his stroke from every side. The background landscape is painted on to a plastic strip affixed to the back of the dome. And it's not just snowflakes that come raining down, it's golf balls too. Watch out!

Hoping to shed a few pounds before your vacation? This "before and after" snowdome makes it seem like a cinch. All you have to do is step through to the other side of the looking glass. Perhaps this proves the power of positive thinking.

BEFORE AND AFTER

For the male counterparts, just like in a circus side show, one look in the magic mirror miraculously transforms the ninety-nine-pound weakling into an instant body-building champ. In the 1950s, there were famous ads on the topic. Perhaps this dome was inspired by them.

BEFORE AND AFTER

What could be a more natural setting for this expert figure skater than a winter wonderland decorated only with tiny flakes of snow? This recent model, made by Koziol, has an inventive addition. The skater's hair and outfit are invisibly textured so as to catch the snow without it sliding off.

Snowdomes make a perfect gift on any occasion. This tennis tableau is inscribed on the back with a "Good Luck" message. As such, it is an ideal lucky charm to give before a match, or before an important meeting or interview. For added good wishes, balls rain down alongside the shiny metallic snowflakes.

With a hose over his shoulder and an ax in hand, this brave New York fireman is off to the rescue. Embedded within the beautifully wrought base are the various tools and symbols that represent his trade.

Ussé is one of those castles in the Loire Valley of France that seem to come right out of a fairy tale. Although it was largely rebuilt in the fifteenth and sixteenth centuries, it retains a medieval dungeon. The court jester in his bubble could probably regale us with many a tale of heroic exploits on the part of the chivalrous knights who would have jousted within the castle walls in days gone by.

The bigtop provides a regular three-ring circus full of lively snowdome subjects. Are the fire eater and snake charmer man and wife, or just companions of circumstance? By the looks of her expression, she seems more worried for him than for herself.

*The blonde assistant seems utterly
fearless, under fire from the
blindfolded knife-thrower. Perhaps
she knows that that "all the world's
a stage," as Shakespeare said. Or
maybe she realizes that this is just a
snowdome she's caught in.*

Money doesn't make for happiness, so the saying goes. But it seems that the fellow in this snowdome hasn't heard. Knee-deep in a pile of greenbacks, he raises his arms in sheer joy. Or perhaps it is his way of asking for more. Just a flick of the wrist and dollars come raining down upon him.

Is this some extraterrestrial baby from Mars? Or some kiddy figurine about to become the next Pokémon? What it most resembles, perhaps, are the famous Nana sculptures of Niki de Saint-Phalle. Inflatable Saint-Phalle souvenirs can sometimes be found in a museum shop. But this one, if it is a Saint-Phalle, does not have the artist's authorization.

Although snowdomes are not often found in Africa, the continent still proved inspirational for this design: and these three dancing warriors don't seem to feel the cold.

This African king's mask, surrounded by leopard-skin totems, shows off quite a smile. This seems fitting as "Africa" comes from the greek word phriké, *the country where it is never cold. In this snowdome, the snowflakes are replaced by a shower of golden glitter.*

In the generally inoffensive universe of snowdomes, this globe is a rare exception. It was made to advertise a pornographic movie called Citizen Shane, a clear allusion to Orson Welles' Citizen Kane. In Welles' film, there is a paperweight at the very beginning. Maybe that's the connection.

The low level of the water here demonstrates the magnifying effect that the water has on its subject: the body appears disproportionately large in relation to the head.

With his head in the clouds like a god, and rising above the Eiffel Tower, here is the famous French designer Jean-Paul Gaultier, portrayed by the photographer team Pierre et Gilles.

This collector's item was produced in an edition of 3,000 in 1990, to accompany the publication of a book by the great Gaultier.

Another rarity by the same artists, Pierre et Gilles, this two-faced snowdome was made in the year 2000 for the opening of an art show on the theme of beauty. To the left, on a pinkish background with glittering flecks instead of snow, is the artists' vision of the Hindu deity Krishna.

To the right, in the costume and pose of a belly dancer, comes the Pierre et Gilles rendition of Lisa Maria. In fact, the snowdome is a perfect format for these highly imaginative, colorful artists' esthetics. And what better idea than a two-sided model?

Perhaps whoever made this irreverent snowdome should keep quiet about their identity. Otherwise, they might get into trouble with censorship from some moral-minded authority.

BOULE DE CRISTAL

SPECIAL VO ANCE

EXTRA MODE

Anatomically speaking, and in every respect perhaps, this model may also be considered suspect. But again, that is a matter of taste. Lovers of the ghoulish may delight in the knowledge that this globe is made of a substance that gives when you poke your finger into it—just like a real eyeball in fact! Perhaps this may explain the ring of burst blood vessels.

Rose-colored glasses, anyone? Perhaps the world is a better place with Marilyn Monroe and Humphrey Bogart filling the horizon of these companion snowdomes. The graphics are cut out from Andy Warhol's immortalizing versions of the stars. And the pink liquid inside is rose water, of course.

This classic Marilyn pose pays tribute to the unforgettable scene from director Billy Wilder's The Seven Year Itch, *when this beauty stands over a Manhattan subway grille on the sidewalk, to catch the only August breeze in town. The air current lifts her skirt, and the rest is history. The film was made in 1955, but the snowdome version is much more recent.*

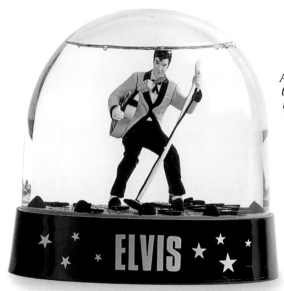

As befits a king—when the king is Elvis, that is—the snowflakes in this dome are replaced with pink sequins and black vinyl albums. In fact, pink and black dominate the scene here, making it pleasingly graphic. And Elvis' pose is convincingly ready for action.

Against the French tricolor flag background stands General Charles de Gaulle. The calendar component of this model has gone irretrievably blank. Otherwise the date would be firmly set on the 18th of June 1940.

"That's one small step for man, one giant leap for mankind." Those were the words spoken by astronaut Neil Armstrong, and heard around the world, by six hundred million television viewers on July 20, 1969, when he stepped on to the moon's surface, the first man to do so. The heroic and historic feat of the Apollo XI crew is surely never to be forgotten, and a fair share of snowdome depictions will help see to that. The globe version on the right has an elaborately detailed base that realistically represents the moon's surface.

II

TRAVELER'S
snowdomes

As a rule of thumb, the more well known a place is as a center of tourism, and the greater the number of visitors who frequent a locality, the more snow-domes and snowglobe versions of it are likely to be made. There are so many specimens on the market that building a collection of location snowdomes calls for a measure of discrimination and some creative decision-making. You might choose to focus on all the different views you can find of one particular city. Or you may want to go for only the most unusual and out-of-the-way spots, particularly those which are represented in a truly realistic manner. Yet again, your sense of irony may lead you to enjoy choosing places where it could never snow in reality.

Paris and New York are probably two of the most popular locations featured in snowdomes. The Arc de Triomphe was commissioned by Napoleon in 1806, but it took thirty years to finish. The monument is shown to a fine advantage in this mint condition 1940s model. The egg-shaped globe contrasts perfectly with the sharp geometrical lines of the bright red base.

A sort of Parisian counterpart to the Statue of Liberty, the Eiffel Tower may win the all-time record for the number of appearances in snowdomes. A 1940s version, with an oval-shaped enclosure like that of the Arc de Triomphe at left, can be seen on page 15. The frame and foliage in this rendition make perfect stopping points for the snowflakes to alight.

Weighing in at a whopping 7,175 tons, the Eiffel Tower was built for the Paris Exposition of 1889. As it was being built many protests against its "ugliness" were made, and the tower was almost dismantled after the world's fair. What a terrible mistake that would have been for tour marketing in France! In this version, the Arc de Triomphe, Notre-Dame Cathedral, and the Sacré-Coeur Basilica, with its distinctive white dome, are all squeezed in for a real bargain.

This little Eiffel Tower is a night view, with glittering blue flakes for a touch of after-dark glamour. The real Eiffel Tower has a roving searchlight on top that arches its periodic way through the Parisian sky. Somebody should invent a battery-powered snowdome that lights up for the same effect. Or maybe they already have.

No, the Eiffel Tower is not the only thing to see in Paris. For many it is not even the main attraction, though the world of snowdomes makes that hard to believe. On one of those famous boat rides along the Seine, you will catch fine glimpses of both the Eiffel Tower and Notre-Dame Cathedral. But the Arc de Triomphe, also pictured here, is a bit more landlocked. In any case, the geography is off. But there are plenty of other ways of looking at it too, as the models on the facing page show.

New York and its Statue of Liberty (see page 102) are all-time favorite snowdome subjects. This version clearly dates from before the Twin Towers tragedy. They appear proudly and prominently in the foreground. Liberty's lamp burns bright red here. Perhaps it has something to do with the city's nickname, the Big Apple.

New York is a place with a lot of heart, and its familiar "I love NY" articulates the word love with a heart symbol. This snowdome echoes that, placing the glorious Manhattan skyline, seen again from the harbor, under a heart-shaped glass.

Here again is a favorite view of the Big Apple skyline, with Miss Liberty dominating the foreground in the harbor. In all its impressive detail, this scene reflects the view that would have greeted passengers on the famous liners that sailed into port hoping to win the coveted Blue Ribbon award for the fastest transatlantic transport.

*New York goes in for a more Hollywood style here, with
the movable boat gliding through the harbor in front of
the Statue of Liberty. Several boat excursions make
hourly and daily tours in the harbor, and some even circle
Manhattan itself, which is not such a big island after all.
This model is more ship-in-a-bottle than snowdome.*

Officially opened on May 27, 1937, San Francisco's Golden Gate Bridge was never golden in color, nor exactly red as it is shown in this snowdome. The actual hue is a deep orange, which is bright enough to stand out even in the notorious San Francisco fog. It takes around forty full-time painters and 5,300 gallons of paint per year to keep it that way.

Perhaps no other famous bridge is quite as different from the Golden Gate as the one in Avignon, in the south of France. According to legend, the Avignon bridge was originally built by a thirteen-year-old shepherd named Bénezet. The boy's idea was to make it easy for pilgrims to reach the city. The poor lad died at the age of twenty, and did not live to see his project completed a few years later, back in 1184.

This French bridge in the sleepy town of Saint-Nazaire on the Loire river is neither famous nor historic. But it makes a fine snowdome subject none-theless. That is due partly to its construction, which is both lofty and sloping, but also perhaps to the dome designer's smart three-quarters take on the scene.

PONT DE SAINT
NAZAIRE-ST BREVIN

If you're in Venice, you'll want to ask this gondolier to take you to the Bridge of Sighs. This romantic walkway was built in 1600 to connect the jail to the ruling Doge's Palace. The heart-wrenching sighs of the prisoners wafted up from their damp cells. Among the very few ever to have escaped from this closely guarded dungeon was the famously libido-driven Casanova, who lived to write down his many exploits, including the escapes.

One of the most famous Parisian tourist spots, and a natural snowdome favorite, is the Sacré-Coeur Basilica, perched above the city high in the northern Montmartre section. The basilica's fairy-tale domes seem tailor-made to fit under curved glass, and the complex's unearthly whiteness itself appears to have been conceived with a coating of snow in mind. But construction got started in the 1870s, before snowdomes were invented.

This vintage glass snowglobe also holds a replica of the Sacré-Coeur Basilica, only its processional stairways and terraces are missing, which gives the structure an almost Gothic, eerie feel. This is heightened by the fact that the liquid has leaked out, removing the magnifying effect. The basilica is made from a special kind of stone that actually whitens with age. But this version seems to have gone prematurely gray.

A huge tourist attraction of the coast of France, Mont Saint-Michel has a selection of dozens of different snowdome and snowglobe souvenirs for the visitor to choose from. In fact a whole collection could be built around representations of the abbey and its surrounding buildings. Aside from variations in coloring, there are those with and without boats, those that double as calendars, as here, those that serve as hourglasses or egg timers, in plastic or real glass, tapered, or rounded, and so on.

This pretty model is typical of the 1940s lines. In the early days, before things were a bit more standardized, lots of different materials were tested for the "snow" part of snowdomes. Among the imaginative choices were crushed sea urchin shells, bone shards, bits of ceramic, and wax mixed with camphor. Judging from the heaviness and color of the sparkles in this model, they are probably made of copper.

*La Chapelle Montligeon is a charming
out-of-the-way spot in northern
France. It may no longer have
a chapel in the conventional
sense, but, as you can see
from this splendid Gothic
Revival-style basilica, it
certainly has an imposing
place of worship. There
are roughly two hundred
French place names
with the word
"chapelle" in them.
They alone could form
the basis for an
impressive snowdome
collection.*

Here is another basilica, much older this time and even more imposing. In fact, Saint Peter's Basilica in Rome is so majestically proportioned, it seems squashed inside this narrow snowdome. Small wonder. The impressive dome of the church is one of the largest in the world, measuring 404 feet (123 m) high with a diameter of 137 feet (42 m). The basilica was completed in 1626.

La Chaise-Dieu is a charming town to the southeast of Paris. The cloister featured in the dome was founded in the eleventh century, and most of the structure dates to the fifteenth century. These days the town is also known for a yearly music festival which takes place at the end of August.

Canterbury, England's largest cathedral, is full of centuries of history. This dwarf version seems to be the work of a cartoon artist. Why not? After all, comic books and the Middle Ages have always gotten on well. And this is the burial place of the Black Prince, a Hundred Years War hero deserving of a Marvel series.

It reads "Barcelona," but a better name might be "Antonio Gaudí, Architect Extraordinaire." This busy snowdome shows two of the architect's masterpieces, both in Barcelona. The orange structure is the Church of the Sagrada Familia, begun in 1884 but still a work in progress. And the seemingly distorted building behind is the Casa Mila, an apartment house built in 1905–1907.

It is said that Saint Patrick used the clover to explain the mystery of the Holy Trinity to his flock. He must have done a fine job judging by these two snowdomes!

Here's the last basilica of this book, Notre-Dame-de-la-Garde in Marseilles, France. If it weren't perched high above the harbor, it might just fall into the sea that surrounds this large port town. Snowdomes in themselves are thoroughly secular objects; it is just that religious monuments look so nice under glass. Then again, snowdome collecting is undeniably a cult for some people.

N.D. DE LA
GARDE/MARSEILL

This ship does bear a prominent cross, but that may be for esthetic reasons, to counterbalance the lighthouse in the foreground. Or it may be a mast without a sail. The location is equally mysterious. Without a sticker to proclaim the name of this seafaring scene, it could take place in any port from the Atlantic to the Pacific.

This twin ship, rectangular model could be representing a sailing regatta of tall ships, or the World's Cup. It is a prototype that never went into production, perhaps because snowdomes should not look like aquariums. Note the stopper at the top for convenient refilling.

The lovingly painted image in this 1940s model is two-dimensional, with important details, such as the breaking waves and parasols, represented in slight relief. The other side, decorated with equal patience and detail, also shows two boats and a lighthouse, but instead of the beach and its parasols there is a rocky, wild coast, with trees.

*Many snowdomes are hand-painted, so that no two are
actually identical, if you look up close. The orange sails
and red flags on this ship make it look rather exotic, as
if it is headed for a deserted South Seas island. But if
you keep your eyes open and have some luck, you may
just find the same ship sailing under different colors.*

With its clever allusion to the tradition of miniature ships in bottles, this snowdome in the round seemed like a good idea to someone. The only problem is that it won't stop rolling on its side, unless it is propped into position. And standing it on its flat end would ruin all the fun. But maybe it is meant to be held in your hand.

This dome comes with an easily removable refill stopper so that it can be refilled with distilled water as it evaporates. Tour operators, boating companies and even gift shops can order snowdomes like this one and have whatever they wish emblazoned on the plastic tag.

Sometimes calendar snowdomes like this one can be refilled. Through the slot at the back of the base, you can see if the dome has a little plug. If it does, twist the dome very gently to detach it from the base. Don't twist it too hard though or it could break.

*This "snowbottle" has flat sides, enabling it
to stay in place, unlike the one on page 169.
Another novelty of sorts is the fact that it contains
exactly the same scene, on
inspection, as the one
pictured on the
facing page.*

SAINT MALO

Saint Malo was known for its swashbuckling pirates, so the treasure chest does make a fitting memento. But this casket motif caught on so well, that it was used for other, less appropriate models. Perhaps this tiny treasure chest doesn't even count as a snowdome.

SAINT MALO

The shell base is entirely appropriate for maritime snowdome and snowglobe themes. This sort of decoration was most commonly found in Italy, making it likely that this beguiling scene comes from there. Generally, to the dismay of collectors and would-be collectors, snowdomes don't come labeled with the manufacturer's name and location.

This is against international trade regulations, but something you can apparently get away with in the souvenir industry. It allows middlemen to stand between snowdome makers and retailers and makes for easier distribution of similar models in different places. The scenery, too, can be fairly anonymous.

BARFLEUR

Another case of strange, interchangeable snowdome décor. This scene of Menton pictures a calm schooner on a placid stretch of sea, in a green bay surrounded by majestic trees. But look at the strange boat on the right and you'll notice the two vessels are almost the same.

This one sways on a seesaw, and the background is more lively, with jaunty palm trees and a three-toned rainbow. But otherwise, these Chinese-made models are so alike they could switch places. Realism? How often does it snow on a Californian beach?

This somber dome shows London's Tower Bridge which is not to be confused with the one in the nursery rhyme "London Bridge is Falling Down." This London bridge was built in 1885 and has been standing ever since. It is the only bridge over the river Thames in London that can be raised to let ships pass, as it is doing here.

TOWER BRIDGE
LONDON

Niagara Falls is like a miracle of natural hydraulics, as well as a traditional honeymoon destination. This 1930s snowglobe doubles as an ample ashtray, with a black Bakelite base. Even the liquid inside is frothing up, as if to participate in the picture.

Souvenir of
Niagara Falls, N. Y.

Gambling was first legalized in the state of Nevada in 1946, which is something of a shame, because it means that there is a dearth of Las Vegas snowdomes before this date. What better subject matter for a colorful universe under glass than these extravagantly decked out casinos? And there is the irresistible temptation to throw dice in, with or without the snow.

In addition to being a seaside resort, Atlantic City is also known for its gambling casinos. The casket form of this snowdome is for those who want to hit it big and need somewhere to stash all their cash. The handy treasure chest has a transparent lid, so it can be seen from above, just as if you were passing over on the way to New York by plane.

The year 2000 was a time for celebration, and what better spot for a deluxe snowglobe commemoration than Times Square in New York, where the ball drops at midnight? For 2000, a new ball was made by Waterford crystal; that must be why it is so large here. The base, with its busy cityscape, is also a music box. It probably plays "Auld Lang Syne".

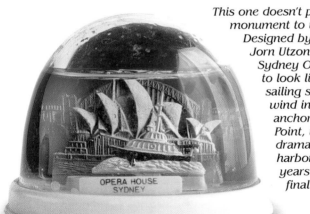

This one doesn't play tunes, but it is a
monument to the human voice.
Designed by the Danish architect
Jorn Utzon, the spectacular
Sydney Opera House is meant
to look like an immense
sailing ship, with the full
wind in its sails. Safely
anchored on Bennelong
Point, the building extends
dramatically into the
harbor. It took fourteen
years to build, and was
finally opened in 1973.

By day or night, Frank Lloyd Wright's Solomon Guggenheim Museum is an unmistakable Manhattan landmark. Wright's designs were not faithfully executed, and he died before the project's completion. But a late 1990s restoration of the Guggenheim building brings it closer in line with the original plans. And these two snowdomes look as though they were based on Wright's drawings.

The Guggenheim is more than a museum; it is a work of art. By the same token, Michelangelo's David is more than just a sculpture, it is a symbol of its native Florence, where it is displayed today in the Galleria dell'Accademia. There are two more copies of David in Florence, one in front of the old city hall, and one on a hill overlooking the city. But you already have your own copy here, under glass.

Ferdinand Cheval was a postman in a French village. Every day on his route, he would stop to pick up pebbles, in order to build, over the course of thirty-three years (1879–1912) his "ideal palace," memorialized here under snow. In 1969, it was officially declared a national monument.

Versailles is another, much bigger French palace; one you're more likely to have heard of. After the Eiffel Tower, it is the most visited monument in France. The tiny medallion layout can't do justice to its grandeur, but it does provide an interesting perspective on the statue of King Louis XIV, with the royal chapel to the right.

The Loire Valley in France is full of fairy-tale castles. It would be a collector's dream to get a complete series of châteaux snowdomes. This particular one is of the Château of Amboise, a sumptuous reconstruction of a medieval fortress, the Tower of Minimes.

AMBOISE

You are looking at the rear of
the French Château of Angers
in this older snowglobe
model. That is why it seems
so grim and fenced in, like
a back yard. If you turn the
globe around, though, it
generously offers you
another perspective of the
castle; the façade that looks
on to the Loire river.

*Made in Hong Kong in the late 1960s, this snowdome
is in good condition, but the scene looks like a view
of Mars, if not some more exotic planet. In fact, it is a
rather fanciful rendition of stalactites in a grotto,
dreamed up by someone who may have never seen a
stalactite, or a grotto for that matter. That is the
beauty of it all.*

ARCY SUR CURE

Here we have a fairly faithful view of the port of Bonifacio, in Corsica. It looks like a charming place to stay, with great swimming and boating, a lovely village, and an impressive ancient citadel on the hilltop. But the stick-on image takes all the fun out of it being a snowdome.

The shells on the pedestal make this snowglobe a typically Italian job. But no need to jump to conclusions: the leaning building is not the Tower of Pisa after all. It is part of some other lovely town in Italy, probably a tranquil spot far from the danger of earthquakes. How did the building get its tilt, then? In fact, the whole scene is on a slant, due to the conjunction of low-tech manufacturing and time.

The little Italian village on a promontory, with its medieval ramparts and fortifications, and its castle on the hill, make for a perfect tourist's dream. But the snowglobe rendition has some technical drawbacks. For example, the blue paint has all flaked off and mixed in with the snow. This makes the whole scene seem like it is covered in heavy haze. How would you ever see your way to the top?

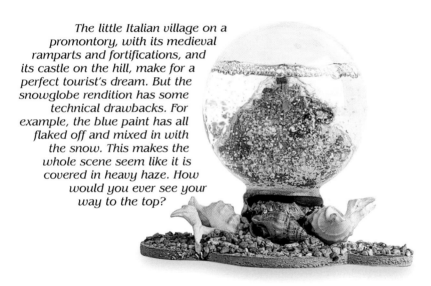

As souvenir items, snowdome manufacturers and tourist sites go in for different strategies. While some snowdomes present recognizable landmarks, others display more emblematic themes. Snowdomes that are souvenirs of large geographical regions, seashores, or mountainsides often take this tack.

Some experts suggest that we can't always blame the use of generic snowdome models on the money-saving measures of the place where they are purchased. They explain that there are some places with nothing special to remember them by!

*These miniature snowglobes both depict something worth
remembering, without a doubt, but they have a particularly
generic charm, all the same. That village on the left could be
nestled beside a mountain stream, or by the sea. As for the house
on the right, it is obviously a ski chalet. But where, exactly, the
Rocky Mountains, Vermont, the Alps? Take your pick.*

No, it isn't the fault of an out-of-focus camera. All the flurry of blurred commotion is due to a battery-run windmill whirring away under glass. The windmill propels a lifetime supply of tiny Styrofoam snowballs.

Things are much clearer in this scene, with a fine sense of perspective, even if it is in the middle of a snowstorm. The graceful swans in the foreground stand out in high relief. In the middle distance, the river Thiou sweeps majestically around the island palace, with the town just behind following the river banks. The mountains you see in the background are the Alps, painted in for good measure.

Here we are high up in the Swiss Alps, with all the classic national symbols that stand out even in a snowstorm like this one. You can make out the tall, snow-covered peak, a cow, a shepherd sounding his horn, and, in the center of it all, the Swiss flag.

What more perfect spot to take off your skis and go inside for a hot chocolate beside a roaring fire? But where are we, exactly? Once again, it could be the Rockies, or northern New England, or the Alps, or even somewhere in Chile, for that matter. But not knowing where it is makes it all more dreamy and cozy.

Maybe it is all this traveling around that leaves us in a whir, or at least blurs our vision. We can tell from the name tag that this is definitely Amsterdam. And, knowing that, the narrow houses with their pointy roofs and windows make sense. But what is that thing that looks like an igloo? Maybe a barge? Or perhaps it is a dam, to remind us of how the town got its name: dam on the river Amstel.

Made by Koziol, a
major German
manufacturer in the
field, these two
snowdomes have
some things in
common, such as
the tiered landscape,
the animal figure,
and the evergreens.
But no one would
mistake them for
the same spot.

There is, however, a winter version available for the village on the left, and a summer scene for the one on the right. But fall and spring are nowhere in sight. The idea has probably crossed someone's mind, though, and it can only be a question of time.

Also by Koziol, a past master of the serial, these souvenir snowglobes of Vienna are incrementally varied. You can choose your rendition of Saint Stephen's Church in a variety of sizes. On the far right is the famous Prater Ferris wheel memorialized in the movie The Third Man. *It was built in 1897 to mark the fiftieth anniversary of the coronation of Emperor Franz Josef of Austria.*

Looking something like a cartoon in this portrayal, the Vasa is a Swedish royal navy ship that sank in the port of Stockholm in 1628, just after setting sail on its maiden voyage. The ship was stocked with sixty-four cannons, but as the weight was unevenly distributed, tragedy struck. After spending 333 years underwater, the vessel was hoisted back up in 1961. It was thoroughly restored and is now its own museum.

STOCKHOLM

The little mermaid of Copenhagen appears with a more subdued color scheme on page 63. What could be the reason behind this wild, fluorescent green background and the screaming fuchsia pedestal? Perhaps some attempt to update the little mermaid. Or maybe it's to remind us of the graffiti that keeps covering the statue.

Innsbruck is the Tyrolean capital where two Winter Olympic Games were held, first in 1964 and again in 1976. This sweet little depiction is miniature even for a snowglobe.

Innsbruck

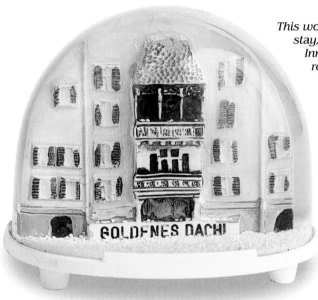

This would be a nice place to stay, if you are going to Innsbruck. But the rooms are not for rent. Goldenes Dachl means "little golden roof." It is a two-story oriel window with an overhanging roof made of 2,714 gold-plated copper shingles.

Completed in 1496, it was built as an addition to the Ducal Palace of Innsbruck.

Valberg is a ski resort in the southern Alps. But the name could have been written in with magic marker by anyone. Yes, those are some tall mountains in the distance. But what does the hungry wolf have to do with it? This could be a scene from the tale of "The Boy Who Cried Wolf," or "Little Red Riding Hood," even.

VALBERG

This time, the scene itself can be changed. In fact, this model is designed for you to slip in a picture of your sweetheart, or a romantic reminder of yourself for your beloved. That is the reason for the square photo format. And of course, it is the logic behind the balloon-like hearts that drift with the snowflakes.

Night and day, may seem, well, as different
as night and day. Perhaps that's so, but this
snowdome pair shows how they can go
hand in hand. Day goes out of her way to
compromise, shining in the dark of night.

In fact, these models use the same tinted blue glass used for Nefertiti on page 103, though her husband was something of a sun worshipper. Unlike the sun, the moon doesn't shine all alone. There are stars in the background.

It looks like either the sun or the moon in the celestial background, but this planet, if that is what it is supposed to be, doesn't quite resemble anything in our solar system. Maybe it is from another galaxy, one where green Silly Putty grows through a Lucite ring from a fiery mound. Is that a sign of intelligent life?

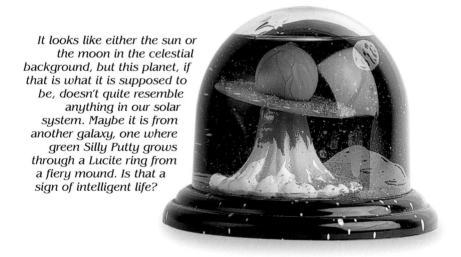

Life on earth doesn't always seem that intelligent either. If we're so smart, why can't we figure out a really effective way to stop polluting the planet and keep the ozone layer from disappearing? This bottle-shaped model paints a grim picture of the situation. But it also offers a clever solution. If only all the smog in Los Angeles could be hermetically sealed in containers and sold as souvenirs to tourists, it could definitely help matters.

III

ANIMAL

snowdomes

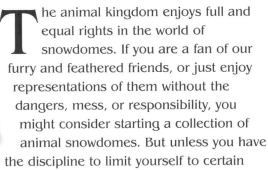

T he animal kingdom enjoys full and equal rights in the world of snowdomes. If you are a fan of our furry and feathered friends, or just enjoy representations of them without the dangers, mess, or responsibility, you might consider starting a collection of animal snowdomes. But unless you have the discipline to limit yourself to certain species only, your collection could start multiplying like bunny rabbits. There is really a lot out there to choose from among all the mammals, fish, reptiles, and birds that have found themselves encased in glass.

The tiny seahorse dipping his snout in a big scallop shell seems lost in concentration. He calls to mind a hummingbird drinking nectar. Maybe he is feasting on a huge helping of fresh scallop sushi. He is so busy that he doesn't notice the blue jewel. But perhaps he is gazing on a whole treasure trove of sapphires.

Swimming upstream with great determination and vigor, this salmon would make a prize catch for any fisherman. But where to seek him out? The tall fir trees on the banks suggest it might be somewhere like Norway or Canada.

Saint-Vaast-la-Hougue is a
port on the French side of
the English Channel, so it is
surprising that this fish
and his vegetarian snack
have such a tropical air
about them. Still, the
basic maritime idea is
clear. This snowdome,
like many, was made
in China, where
perhaps they could
better research
their designs.

Handsome and exotic, sure to be a hit with the opposite sex, this fish nevertheless looks lonely and even depressed. On closer inspection, it appears to be hooked, which could explain its dejection. But there is no need to panic. The wire simply holds the fish to the base, so it can sway with the waves when the snowdome is agitated.

The elaborate plastic dolphin and wave motif are perfect for Marineland, with its live dolphin shows. Inside the globe, another dolphin is gracefully jumping the hoop. The seesaw makes the act look more convincing, animated— and difficult!

And here's our dolphin again, this time at Saint Malo, a French seaside resort. In fact if you look back to pages 172 and 173, you'll see that this is the same Saint Malo scene in yet another package. But it gets worse for the overworked dolphin, whose irresistible cuteness has led him to frame even landlocked tourist destinations.

Despite its shape, this is something of a New Age style of snowdome, with magical, mystical silver dolphins adrift like jeweled clouds on the most tropical of warm seas—or is that the sky? Perhaps there is no difference. And it goes to show that a dolphin is never out of place in eternity.

Here, the ever popular, marvelously serene dolphin seems to be taking a sun bath in a snowstorm. This recent model is a top-quality one of its kind, and supposedly absolutely leakproof. The careful painting and the detailed ceramic base can bring a smile to anyone's face.

Lucky alligators. What better cause for jumping up and down for joy than a vacation in sunny Cuba? The papa alligator holds a perfect Havana cigar in his hand, the kind you had better not try smuggling to the States. The scene is made from a simple flat strip (see page 86).

Maybe this bloated alligator should look at the "before and after" snowdomes on pages 114 and 115 to pick up some fitness tips. It seems it has swallowed two whole baby alligators for breakfast, but the little ones don't seem to mind. They are contentedly seesawing away. The label says "Florida," but an identical "New Orleans" model exists.

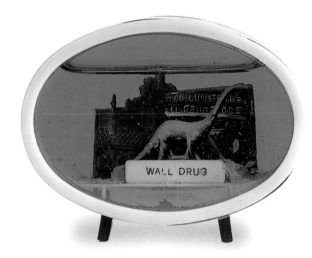

Does a dinosaur really make good advertising for a drugstore? Well, if you were to see this monster ambling toward you, you might hurry inside. This snowdome also exists with the same design, but in a more classic display on a black base.

Is this the Loch Ness monster, who turns out to be friendly after all and gives rides to bathing beauties? But the woman, too, is gigantic in comparison with the sailboat. Maybe it is a toy sailboat then? The monster looks pretty inflatable himself, on second thought—the kind of thing you could pick up in a store for some summer fun.

Penguins are perfectly at home in the cold and windy world of snowglobes. Even the little ones don't seem to mind the weather in this happy, orange-beaked family. This nicely detailed yet simple model is typical of the productions of Koziol, a quality German manufacturer. Just compare the penguins' pared-down, clean style with the figure skater on page 116, also made by Koziol.

In contrast, snow is not the natural habitat for panda bears, despite their thick fur coats. These pandas come from China and are rendered in painstaking detail. As these bears are an important part of Chinese culture, there is little chance for error in this design (see pages 246 and 247).

A tigress' stripes seem to be there for purely esthetic reasons, but of course they serve as camouflage in her natural habitat. You can get a sense of that in this snowdome, partly because of fortuitous damage over time. It is quite difficult to actually pick the great cat out against the savanna landscape.

In case you were about to have doubts as to his presence, this ferocious tiger makes two appearances, one on the outside of the dome and one inside it. The inner, calmer tiger, has a bit more of a mane, upon close inspection. Perhaps this feline ambiguity is deliberate, so that the manufacturer can dress up this model as a lion for another two-in-one effect.

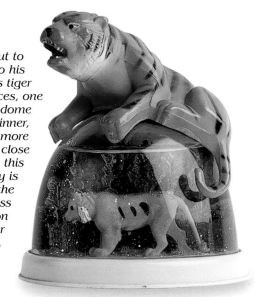

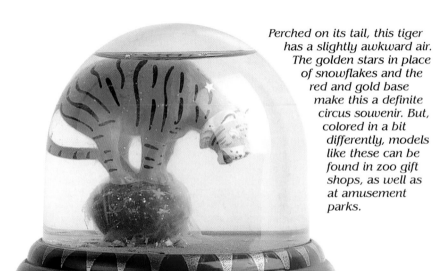

Perched on its tail, this tiger has a slightly awkward air. The golden stars in place of snowflakes and the red and gold base make this a definite circus souvenir. But, colored in a bit differently, models like these can be found in zoo gift shops, as well as at amusement parks.

Straddling the dome, this gorilla seems to be on her guard. Maybe she is an overprotective mother, making sure nothing can harm her young ones, blithely playing on the seesaw inside. But are these in fact her babies? They look suspiciously like dogs. In the dreamy world of snowdomes, perhaps they are imaginary creatures from some far-off mythical land.

A case of mistaken identities? It clearly says "Calais,"
the name of an English Channel port in northern France.
But isn't that an elephant standing in front of the
Forbidden City in China? Unless someone pays more
attention, the elephant will never be trained to catch
those movable rings on its trunk.

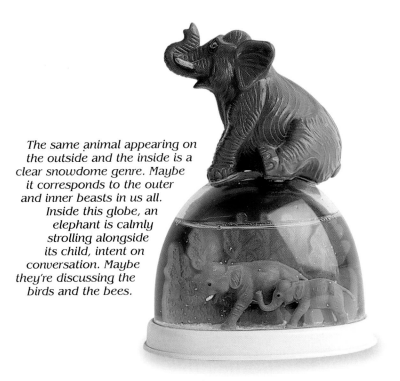

The same animal appearing on the outside and the inside is a clear snowdome genre. Maybe it corresponds to the outer and inner beasts in us all. Inside this globe, an elephant is calmly strolling alongside its child, intent on conversation. Maybe they're discussing the birds and the bees.

Animals are often shown behind
bars too, in a zoo setting. It is
a shame to stick a beautiful
polar bear in a cage, once
he's already under glass.
But this way, the children
in the dome with him are
safe to look on, with
their colorful balloons.
Not all zoos have polar
bears; this must be a
good one. The missing
sticker would tell us
where for certain.

Here's a slice of life from the great outdoors, North Pole style. A grownup polar bear helps a baby polar bear over an ice floe. In a world made all of white, with shimmering snow falling everywhere, you can imagine that it might be hard to find your way. But polar bears learn to get used to all that.

Amid all the lions, tigers, and bears on display under glass, possibly the most frightening animal in the bunch is this gigantic squirrel, which towers over the huge evergreen trees. Perhaps the snowdome designer has a strange sense of perspective.

In a somewhat more convincing scenario, a chamois bounds over the foothills, with impressive snow-covered mountains in the distance. Their deep gulleys would make great ski slopes—but only for daredevils and highly experienced athletes.

The Clydesdale horses pulling the buggy are the trademark of the Anheuser Busch brewing company. And this 1960s snowdome serves as advertising for the firm. The flattened oval shape was certainly a novelty in the world of snowdomes (see also page 228).

The red geometrical base and egg-shaped globe are trademarks of Ets C. & Cie, a French snowdome manufacturer that operated all too briefly in the 1940s. Careful attention to detail is typical of this company. The boar in this tableau is a fine example of the artistry exhibited in all its products.

In Arctic regions there are
of course reindeer, but
what are those strange
mushrooms growing
to the left? We hope
that the figure
holding the sign is a
totem pole, rather
than a man frozen
to the spot.

The dogsled and bear totem make this a fitting representation of Alaska, especially with all the snow added. The figure on the right is dwarfed by his dogs, the mountains are eerily yellow, and the perspective a bit wacky, but nobody's perfect. Are we in Juno or Anchorage, or Fairbanks, or Ketchikan...?

A cow is a fitting symbol for Normandy, a region of France celebrated for its cheeses and dairy products. But the typical Normandy cow is not brown and white; in fact it has a coloring much closer to that of the bull pictured on the facing page. And the head is strangely reminiscent of a dog's.

As for the famous Pamplona bull, the star of the show in the bull-running festivities on San Fermin every summer, he is looking awfully cow-like here. And Pamplona—no seaside resort—would be better represented with its fortress and cathedral in the distance. But with all the shaking of those snowflakes, anyone can get confused.

Pigs can be symbols of sloppiness and the messiest of eaters. These two don't give that impression. The one on the left seems to be an upstanding Midwesterner, the one on the right, a sweet tooth.

There are about as many pig snowdomes as there are domes of any other kind of animal. All this sweet farm needs is a couple more cute piglets.

*From Korean wedding mementos through hunters'
decoys to duck pictures on walls, there are innumerable
duck collectibles. Those who aim for a truly
comprehensive collection should not forget to turn their
sights to snowdomes. Note the rare realistic dignity in
which these ducks have been rendered.*

*Strangely, in the
snowdome world,
roosters are relatively
uncommon compared
with ducks, storks, and
flamingos. This one is
a proud, well-fed, and
finely painted specimen.*

This flamingo dome has become a real collector's item. It was a souvenir at the 1990 American Booksellers' Association convention and is actually a game. You can spend hours trying to get the hoops around the bird's neck. Other snowdome hoop games appear on pages 80, 222, and 236.

Funny that this snowdome has lost its descriptive label. Still, you can find the same model in Florida, northern Africa, and southern France.

This snowdome has also been spotted with a variety of labels, most from eastern France. Note the zoo-like habitat represented in the background.

Here a yellow parakeet contemplates the interesting glass-bound haunt of his fellow creatures. The glass does not contain the usual three-dimensional plastic decor. The inside is made of plastic-coated cardboard and the outside has been hand-painted.

OISEAUX

Owl plumage is
particularly soft and
fluffy. This enables it to
fly quietly in the night.
You can tell that this
miniature model contains
a baby owl because a
little crest is just
beginning to grow on
the chick's head.

These are definitely owl chicks. The owl is the mascot of Athens, Greece. Until the arrival of the Euro there was even a Greek coin that was called by that name because it had a little owl on one side.

*If you encounter a snowdome like this one you have
to consider whether you want your collection to
include examples where so much more is happening
outside the glass globe than in it.*

Here we're reminded once again how folk art and the classics make such a good mix in the world of the snowdome.
Is there a better way of evoking Tchaikovsky's Swan Lake *without watching the ballet or listening to the music?*

This dog is sitting in the mountain pastures of south-central France. He's probably meant to be a sheepdog but resembles a Saint Bernard.

Mont.Dore Sancy

Besse

A monument to shopping and the shopper's best friends. Whether or not bags like these are the result of advertising strategies by a bag manufacturer or a department store, who could deny their practicality and usefulness?

The way to say bear in German is Bär, and the symbol of Berlin is the bear. Here we have a teddy-bear version. The city of Berne in Switzerland and the Urseren Valley both take their names from the bear, too. (The word for bear in Latin is ursus.) You can find snowdome bears in these places as well.

Is it Winnie the Pooh? If so there couldn't be two of him. Is it Paddington? Maybe it's Winnie and Paddington, both in the uniform of Buckingham Palace guards.

We end this chapter with this marvelous penguin and mouse Christmas model, to take you from the animal world to the world of commemorative snowdomes.

Christmas snowdomes have been doing brisk business in the United States and then the rest of the world since the 1960s, so the variety is almost infinite. Some of them are shown on the following pages.

December

Good Housekeeping

25 Cents

30¢ IN CANADA

IV

COMMEMORATIVE

snowdomes

There are so many Santa Claus snowdomes that—as Nancy McMichael put it in her book (see Bibliography)—he can be considered the patron saint of snowdomes. As it turns out, the first Christmas snowdomes were made by the German company, Koziol, in the 1930s. But by the 1950s the number of American Christmas domes far exceeded those produced in all other countries combined. And why not celebrate other occasions as well? After Christmas, why not Easter? And Halloween? In addition to holidays, you will find celebrations of the invention or anniversary of cartoon characters, the release of movies, the Olympic Games, small- and large-scale advertising campaigns—and even the arrival of extraterrestrial spaceships.

Classical and religious themes have long been popular with snowdome makers. Here we have a traditional Adoration of the Kings scene, with Jesus, Mary, Joseph, and the Magi—though there are no animals and King Balthazar is a white man.

Here baby Jesus is visited by angels. In his poem The Magi, W. B. Yeats described the angels' "helms of silver hovering side by side," and "their eyes still fixed, hoping to find once more … the uncontrollable mystery on the bestial floor." But the silver he refers to has more to do with halos than with synthetic snow!

There are innumerable snowdomes featuring the Nativity. On the left is a scene that is serenity itself: a "babe wrapped in swaddling clothes lying in a manger" (Luke 2:12). The manger rises protectively around the snowglobe. On the facing page the snowdome has an elaborate and highly modeled base that doubles as a music box.

*Models like this one
cannot properly be called
snowdomes. They feature
angels, and when you
shake them gold stars,
sequins, or glitter
sprinkle down.*

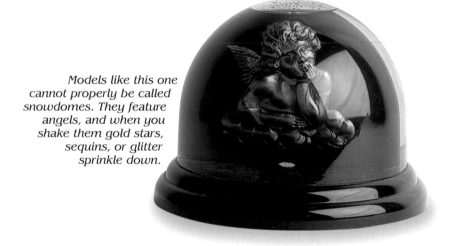

This charming folk-art Santa is made of wood. His snowglobe belly reveals gingerbread Santas and milk cartons. But good little girls and boys will have to wait until Christmas to find out what's in his sack!

- 273 -

Santa Claus or Old Saint Nick is usually called Father Christmas in England, Weihnachtsmann in Germany, Babbo Natale in Italy, Père Noël in France, and el Papá Noel or San Nicolàs in Spanish-speaking countries.

The popularity of the Santa Claus tradition originated with the growth of the Dutch community in North America in the seventeenth century. For them, he was called Kriss Kringle *or* Sint Nikolaas. *The name "Santa Claus" derives from contracted pronunciation of the latter.*

Santa Claus became the internationally popular and recognizable figure he is today thanks to Thomas Nast. Nast was a caricaturist at the New York-based Harper's Illustrated Weekly in 1860 when he first depicted Santa Clause in red jacket and pants with white fur cuffs and the large belt. Nast continued drawing the gift-bearing old man for about thirty years. The rest of the country and then many parts of the world gradually joined him in the celebration.

The Santa Claus legend had to develop over time. It wasn't until 1885 that Thomas Nast decided that the Claus residence was on the North Pole. The writer George Webster then added details concerning the house and workshop.

Merry Christmas

But it was the Coca-Cola
Company that sealed
Santa's fate and
established his definitive
form! In a 1931
advertising campaign it
came up with Santa's
happy red-cheeked face
and jolly corpulence.

The artist who first drew the Coca-Cola Santa that became such a hit with the kids—and other companies' advertising strategies—was Haddon Sundblom. Santa's history is not unusual in the annals of snowdome history, since many snowdome themes are like the children of a marriage between cultural phenomena and marketing.

Here, Frosty the Snowman greets collectors with a cheerful "Hi." The Frosty character is based on a book by Ann Bedford. The book was published in 1950. The television special was first aired in 1969.

Europe was resistant to the Americanized version of Saint Nicholas—for a while, anyway. Catholic groups had for years been denouncing the popular image of Santa as heretical when, on December 23, 1951, Santa was burnt in effigy before the Dijon Cathedral in France. But that attitude is now a very distant memory.

It was Americans who created his clothing, physique and homestead, but the origin of Old Saint Nick goes back a very long way. In the fourth century, a Bishop with that name lived in Myra, in southern Turkey. Traces of cults to Saint Nicholas first appear in Russia, then Italy, and reach Germany around the year 1000. His feast day is on December 6.

Nicholas is a patron saint of sailors and children. Presents were traditionally given to children on December 6, until the practice was moved to the day of Christ's birth. Among Protestant populations in Germany, Holland, and Belgium, however, Santa Claus, or Saint Nicholas, still retains his proper feast day.

Snowdomes with Christmas themes abound. You can find models in every shape and size. This one fits nicely within a book format model. When the holiday ends you can close it up and wait for next year.

The lantern-style models on pages 278 to 280 are simplicity itself, whereas the music box model on page 283 is rather complex. Here the windmill runs on electric power. You turn on the vanes to set the snow in motion.

This snowman model is reminiscent of the penguin on pages 264–265. Snowmen are another snowdome favorite, of course, providing myriad opportunities for creativity.

The Christmas tree tradition derives from Germany and eastern France. Queen Victoria and her husband Prince Albert did much to spread the tradition. Albert was of German origin, and each year the arrival and decoration of a tree at Windsor was celebrated with some fanfare—much like the Christmas tree at the White House and the giant tree in New York's Rockefeller Center.

Christmas snowdomes are not exempt from the occasional defects that occur in manufacture. This little penguin inhabits a polluted world.

Glass models are usually manufactured with a higher degree of quality control. In this case, the seal is particularly important because the base is a music box.

This snowman is trapped in an iceberg, with all the facets of a finely chiseled diamond.

The British retail chain Marks
& Spencer came up with this
sugar-dome model a couple
of years ago. Because it can
be opened and the contents
eaten, it creates a real
tension between your
sweet tooth and your
collector's spirit.

Traditions vary throughout the Christian world as to how Easter eggs are supposed to have arrived in their hiding places on Easter Sunday. In some areas it is the Easter bunny that brings them, in others it is a chicken, a rooster, a stork, a fox...

There are fewer Easter snowdomes than Christmas snowdomes, but a great variety of egg and rabbit Easter theme domes are certainly available.

*Here's the perfect
birthday present for a
snowdome collector.
Too bad the candles
can't be lit.*

Birthday models are also legion, from the stripper jumping out of the cake to Porky Pig.

Halloween is another natural subject. Sometimes, on shaking the dome, you will find orange snow, or even leaves. The number of European Halloween models has been rising steeply in recent years.

A form of Halloween has been celebrated in Europe for about three thousand years. In some places, it was connected to the year's end (which was earlier than now) and the beginning of winter. For instance, the Druids put out a sacred fire on that day and lit another, which was to keep away evil spirits for the following year.

All Saints' Day became an official part of the Catholic calendar in 1048, as most of Europe came to abandon earlier festivals relating to the passing of souls between the worlds of the living and the dead. But Gaelic countries, such as Ireland and Scotland, maintained the tradition. Then, as with the Santa Claus tradition, immigration to the United States was instrumental in the development of the holiday's present form.

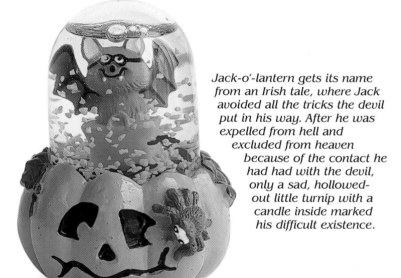

Jack-o'-lantern gets its name from an Irish tale, where Jack avoided all the tricks the devil put in his way. After he was expelled from hell and excluded from heaven because of the contact he had had with the devil, only a sad, hollowed-out little turnip with a candle inside marked his difficult existence.

Halloween is an abbreviated name for All Hallows' Eve (the eve of All Saints), the word hallow itself being a form of "holy." In Irish and Scottish pre-Christian traditions, it was believed that the dead, who normally dwelled on mountaintops, could be perceived on the night of October 31.

People then did their best to try to scare off the dead souls. Halloween costumes were originally meant to keep the dead from haunting the living. The "trick or treat" tradition, where children go from door to door and collect candy, dates to the 1930s.

Traditionally, black cats are witches' companions and may harbor the spirits of humans.

How did witches get into the picture? Legend has it that witches consort with the devil twice a year: on Halloween and on the last day of April. As with many traditions, the various strands of different myths eventually became intermingled and came to influence one another.

*The cat on page 302 seems awfully
sympathetic, a fine companion for the
subject of these three snowdomes of Casper,
the friendly ghost.*

The Halloween shroud-based ghost costume is an English custom. Children would wrap themselves up in old sheets, creep downstairs, and scare all the grown-ups.

Disney has competition from across the Ocean. These two snowdomes come from the Asterix theme park. This one features the rotund figure of Obelix, who tumbled into a pot of magic potion when he was little and now has superhuman strength. Note that he is carrying a wild boar over his shoulder.

Asterix and Obelix were created by René Goscinny in 1959. The "ix" endings of the characters' names, apart from being clever puns, hark back to typical names from Ancient Gaul. And here is Asterix's pooch, Dogmatix. A recent movie increases their international fame.

A snowdome or two can make a fine gift to mark the birth of a child. First the new mother can enjoy it, and the child can enjoy it later—as long as the little one is as well-behaved as these three little angels seem to be!

The "Triplés" trio in fact come from a series of comic strips in a French weekly magazine. Hugely popular in France, they feature not only in snowdomes but in everything from school bags to quilt covers via stationery and T-shirts.

Another European collector's item, this snowdome features Calimero, a chick who owes his birth to an animated advertisement for the laundry detergent Ava. Calimero went on to become internationally famous.

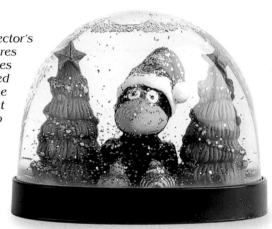

Walt Disney created Mortimer the Mouse in 1929. The next year his name was changed to Mickey. Pluto appeared in 1932 and Donald Duck in 1934. While the characters often appeared together at first, independent cartoon series were soon developed.

Donald usually wore a smock-like shirt that echoed popular children's clothing of the period when he was first created. His jacket, hat, and bow tie here probably mean that he is heading for a date with his girlfriend, Daisy Duck.

Shaky-frames like this one, where you just slide a photograph into the background, were particularly popular in the 1970s. Disney characters often occupied the foreground, especially in the models made by Monogram Products. But many other companies have put similar products on the market and continue to do so. Koziol is one example (see page 211).

*These are Mickey and Minnie snowdome pencils,
available at your closest Disneyland,
Disneyworld, or Disney store. You could
sharpen them up with the little Dutch girl
on page 89.*

Minnie Mouse was created in 1930 when, of course, she was required to wear panties under her dress. She also wore a hat. In 1969 she had a makeover; a bow replaced her hat and she was given long eyelashes. The snowdome at right suggests that Minnie and Mickey had a child, but aren't they an eternal boyfriend-girlfriend couple?

The movie Snow White and the Seven Dwarfs *was Disney's first full-length feature film. When it came out in 1937 it immediately became an international success.*

In addition to developing the dwarfs' characters more than the Grimm fairytale had, the film used 1,200 colors. You won't find quite as impressive an array in Snow White snowdomes, but you will find many different scenes.

Here Bambi meets his friend Pan Pan the rabbit. The two become fast friends and cavort about. The scene where they slide around on the lake remains an unforgettable classic. Walt Disney released the animated film Bambi in 1942.

This calendar snowdome is a more vintage model than the one on the facing page. Besides Bambi, you are bound to come across many other favorite characters from the Disney classics: Alice in Wonderland, Cinderella, Dumbo, Pinocchio, and many more. But beware, there is stiff competition between snowdome and Disney memorabilia collectors.

Disney's Toy Story came out in 1995. You may recognize its heroes, Buzz and Woody. The base is a music box that plays the film's soundtrack.

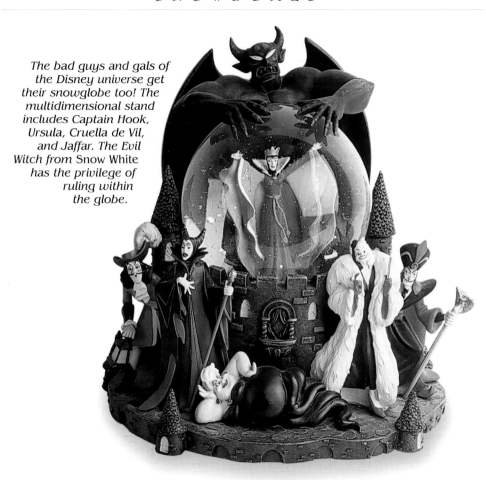

The bad guys and gals of the Disney universe get their snowglobe too! The multidimensional stand includes Captain Hook, Ursula, Cruella de Vil, and Jaffar. The Evil Witch from Snow White *has the privilege of ruling within the globe.*

Disney also produced its version of Little Red Riding Hood. *Originally, it was a cautionary tale to warn young women about wily seducers. When Little Red Riding Hood was made into a much younger girl, the moral was shifted to stress the importance of obedience.*

Compared with the model on the previous page, this one is more substantial but has less charm. In Charles Perrault's version of the story, Little Red Riding Hood carries a container with butter. Here she seems to have a bottle of wine in her basket!

*The birds ate the breadcrumbs that would have
indicated the way home, and Hansel and Gretel
started eating the witch's gingerbread house...
This model and that on the facing page
complement the Red Riding Hood models on
pages 322 and 323.*

Sometimes it takes knowledge of the old classics to recognize a snowdome's theme. This Hansel and Gretel dome gives fewer clues than the version opposite as to its origin as a Grimm brothers tale.

This too represents a character from a Grimm brothers tale, the story of the tailor who proudly makes himself a belt inscribed with, "Seven in one fell swoop." The tailor killed seven flies in one swat. He subsequently embarks on a series of adventures, and eventually becomes king.

Das tapfere Schneiderlein

True fans define themselves in relation to different stages of Batman's glory. Some people swear by the comic strip, which first appeared in 1939. Some people only respect the 1960s television series. Others see the movies of 1989 and 1992 as the apotheosis of Batmanism.

These two pages portray Bart Simpson, hero of The Simpsons *television show. Snowdomes are often hard to date. But Twentieth Century Fox removed all difficulty here by printing the copyright date.*

THE SIMPSONS™

There are also snowdomes featuring other Simpsons characters, including the parents Homer and Marge, Bart's sisters Lisa and Maggie, their dog, and their cat.

THE SIMPSONS™

THE SIMPSONS TM & © 1993
TWENTIETH CENTURY FOX FILM
CORPORATION. ALL RIGHTS RESERVED

This charming lantern model has not been definitively identified. Perhaps it's a version of The Phantom Tollbooth, *or a scene from* Charlie in the Chocolate Factory.

Troll figurines were a kids' favorite in the 1990s. This pink one has been trapped in a snowdome. Troll hairstyles come in several different fluorescent colors. The way this troll's hair floats in the water gives him quite a look.

These two models probably represent some Scandinavian folk character. In any event, they provide an opportunity for comparing different treatments of the same subject.

The one at left has very little relief work in the plastic. The one on this page has more relief and painting detail. Note the shading on the trees. Both models, however, have the same amount of snow.

On the night of July 2–3, 1947, the inhabitants of Roswell in New Mexico reported seeing a shining disk flying in the sky. A few days later, word was circulating that an extraterrestrial vehicle and its navigator had crashed a few miles away.

This paperweight contains a representation of the Roswell extra-terrestrial. The lack of snow may or may not have to do with the fact that the creature never had the opportunity of encountering any in the Nevada desert.

This snowdome commemorates the bicentennial of the French Revolution. It is a symbol of freedom. The conical cap with a dangling peak is called a Phrygian cap, or "cap of liberty," because of its popularity during the French Revolution. Frenchmen and Saxons wore similar caps in the Middle Ages, as did freed slaves in the Roman Empire before them.

A fine commemorative
globe, that places the
Bastille as its
centerpiece. This
medieval fortress in
Paris was stormed and
destroyed by the
revolutionary mob on
July 14, 1789. Note the
brickwork detail. But snow
at the height of summer
seems a little incongruous!

D-Day, on June 6, 1944, was the day of the invasion by Allied American, British, and Canadian forces in northern France whose thrust led to the defeat of the Nazis. The very first place American airborne divisions landed was Sainte-Mère-Eglise, as British troops cut off enemy communications. This dome commemorates the event, and even portrays the paratrooper who spent the entire battle dangling from the church's stonework where his parachute had become tangled.

This dome was made to honor the Atlanta Olympics of 1996, the centennial anniversary of the modern Olympic Games. A total of 197 nations participated.

The French Bank, Crédit Lyonnais, was an official Olympic sponsor of the 1992 Albertville winter Olympic Games. The bank had a number of these snowdomes made, but they are not as sought after as the two on the facing page, with their cheeky little snow imp mascot.

This athlete's name is Magic, the mascot of the Albertville Games. Others of Magic's ilk include Schuss, from the 1968 Grenoble Games, Waldi, the dachshund from the 1972 Munich Games, Schneemann, the snowman from Innsbruck in 1976, and Vushko, the wolf from Sarajevo in 1984.

Claudia Schiffer graces the interior of this snowglobe. While she lent her face to the advertising of the Citroën Xsara, she decided not to participate in the carmaker's filmed crash-test that featured the effectiveness of its airbags.

NOUVELLE CITROËN XSARA HDi

The white rubber French cousin of the Poppin' Fresh Dough Boy is the Michelin symbol, Bibendum. He has been an essential element in Michelin advertisements for tires, and has adorned other Michelin products, such as maps and guides, since 1913.

You may have noticed the tendency among contemporary advertisers to use the classic 1940s snowglobe form, a perfectly round ball or a base. Elle magazine is always at the forefront of fashion trends.

Libération *is a daily tabloid-form French newspaper. Santa seems to be reading a different paper.*

This is Snowman, who features in the children's books of Jacques Duquesnoy. Snowman is a sort of Santa's helper. What better place to publicize a snowman than in a snowdome?

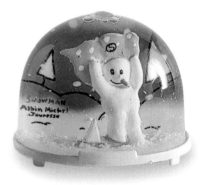

This snowdome advertises the art of advertising itself. The distribution of Bonjour, the French equivalent of the Penny Saver, is indicated by the pink squares on the map of France in the background—a fine visual echo of the tumbling snow.

A radio station decided to take the "snow" in snowdomes literally with these models. Note how the action depicted is not skiing itself, but between-run moments. The views from these ski lifts are spectacular. All that's missing is the soundtrack.

A collector's item for the television lover. France launched its third television station in 1972. At first it was called FR3. In 1992 it was renamed France 3.

The futuristic architecture of this science-oriented theme park, which opened in 1987, is featured inside this dome. This is another true collector's item: the name was later changed to Planet Futuroscope.

This plastic rock is not so heavy, and any individual snow-dome doesn't weigh very much, but the place where you keep or display your snowdomes must be sturdy enough to bear the weight of a growing collection. Remember that water isn't light.

La Villette has a very interesting schedule of fairs, cultural events and a science museum. Most museums now sell their own snowdomes, but some are perhaps more imaginative than this one.

The French postal system put out this snowglobe in its own honor. The airplane resembles those once used by its fleet. A "numéro vert" is a toll-free telephone number.

The colorful comedy, Austin Powers, was released in 1997. The movie reinvented the 1960s for the 1990s, and brought the word "shag" from England to the American vocabulary.

The vast tobacco conglomerate Altadis brought its powerful advertising skills to this snowdome. It also sponsors and produces films.

This souvenir model of Strasbourg also honors one of that city's traditional industries, beer brewering. The object concealed within the blizzard is a traditional ceramic beer-bottle stopper.

The Buddha Bar in Paris is one of the latest shrines of the be-seen ethic. Sprinkling oneself with glitter, like the bar's namesake under glass, may or may not create the desired effect.

Kinder candies have been providing special surprises inside their chocolates since 1975. Kids love them, and many love to collect the surprise gifts as well.

M&Ms have been around
since 1941. Their original
inspiration was
apparently the maker's
encounter with Spanish
soldiers who coated
their chocolate with
sugar. Here the
mysterious green
M&M takes on an
affectionate look.

*Another famous "M".
Richard and Maurice
McDonald opened their
first drive-in restaurant
in 1937. Within seven
years there were
already a hundred of
these double golden
arches throughout
the United States.*

Pulpa is an ice-cream and frozen dessert company. In France, ice-cream cone advertisements call upon sex appeal more frequently than family values or the touting of quality ingredients. You can get a flavor of that in this snowdome.

*Pharmaceutical
companies use all forms
of marketing techniques.
Why leave out the
snowdome?*

Another pharmaceutical company giveaway. You judge the different effect of yellow versus white powder flakes.

When trying to sell a new cosmetic product, what better idea than using the star of snowdomes: the Eiffel Tower. This is a rare example of the association of a product with a historical monument.

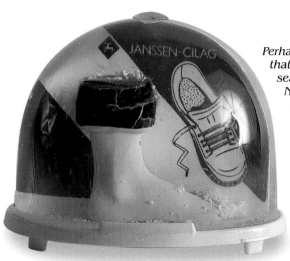

Perhaps it's just as well that this foot remains sealed under glass. No need to worry, though: the company advertising on this page makes products that eliminate foot odor.

Two pieces of advice: remember that a collection of snowdomes may weigh more than you think. Also, it isn't always a good idea to keep your collection in your bedroom, especially the pieces that are easily refillable. Those with simple stoppers sometimes make eerie sounds as air and moisture escape. When refilling, it's best to use distilled water.

And it is with this simple and sweet little German snowdome that I bid you goodbye—and "viel Glück" (good luck) in beginning or developing your collection.

Index,
Bibliography, &
Addresses

Index

The index includes the names of the most important places, subjects, and manufacturers that feature in this book.

INDEX

INDEX

INDEX

Articles about Mireille Sueur and her collection have appeared in several newspapers and magazines. Over the past twenty years she has built a collection of more than two thousand pieces—and the end is definitely not in sight. She is an avid visitor of flea markets, gift shops, and tourist sites. When I met her doing research for this book, her first words of advice were, "Make sure to tell your readers that they should know how to limit themselves." The number of snowdome themes, sizes, and trends is tremendous.

Acknowledgements

I would like most of all to thank Mireille Sueur who gave us free access to her collection. She opened up her home to us, and generously shared with us her time and expertise.

My thanks also extend to Lydia Dailloux, Allan Borvo and Charlotte Pascal, who lent us their snowdomes during the course of the creation of this book, and to Pierre Convert of Établissements Convert, where the photographs for this book were taken.

Thierry Gitton of the Louvre des Antiquaires graciously lent us the sulfide and millefiori paperweights, and Martine Roccard and Claire Ducamp provided invaluable assistance.

Bibliography

Nancy McMichael, *Snowdomes*. New York: Abbeville Press, 1990.

Connie Moore and Harry Rinker, *Snowglobes*. Apple-Courage,1993.

Helene Guarnaccia, *Collector's Guide to Snow Domes*. Paducah, KY: Collector Books, 1994.

Snobiz Magazine, ed. Nancy McMichael, P.O. Box 53262 Washington, DC 20009.

Addresses

Herb Rabbin
Snowdome Repair
PO Box 421205
Los Angeles, CA 90042
USA

Global Shakeup
235 East Colorado Boulevard, # 178
Pasadena, CA 91101
USA
Tel: 323 259 8988
Fax: 323 256 8325

Internet sites

www.heritagestudio.com/snoglobe.htm
web.wt.net~jsims/SnowDomes/snowdomes.htm
www.muntner.com/snowdome.htm
www.snowdome.net/link.html
www.hollyvandyne.com/whatshakin.html
www.sympac.com.au/~redunion/snowdome.htm

In the same series

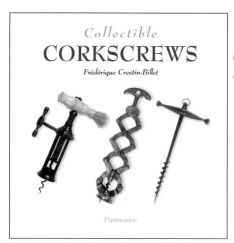

Collectible CORKSCREWS
Frédérique Crestin–Billet

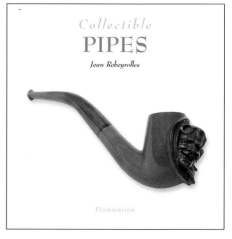

Collectible PIPES
Jean Rebeyrolles

Collectible POCKET KNIVES
Dominique Pascal

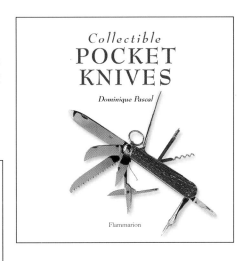

Collectible MINIATURE CARS
Dominique Pascal

Collectible WRISTWATCHES
René Pannier

Collectible FOUNTAIN PENS
Juan Manuel Clark

Collectible MINIATURE
PERFUME BOTTLES
Anne Breton

Photographic credits

*All color photos are by Antoine Pascal
and are part of the
Archives & Collections series.
e-mail: archives.collections@wanadoo.fr
Copyright reserved for all other documents.*

FA0889-02-VI
Dépôt légal: 06/2002